Follow Me Arou Germany

By Wiley Blevins

Content Consultant: Colin Benert, PhD, Lecturer in German, Director of Undergraduate Studies, Department of Germanic Studies, University of Chicago, Chicago, Illinois

Library of Congress Cataloging-in-Publication Data
Title: Germany / by Wiley Blevins.
Description: New York, NY : Children's Press, 2018. | Series: Follow me around | Includes bibliographical references and index.
Identifiers: LCCN 2017030753 | ISBN 9780531234563 (library binding) | ISBN 9780531243688 (pbk.)
Subjects: LCSH: Germany—Juvenile literature. | Germany—Description and travel—Juvenile literature.
Classification: LCC DD17 .B55 2018 | DDC 943—dc23
LC record available at https://lccn.loc.gov/2017030753

Design: Judith Christ Lafond & Anna Tunick Tabachnik
Text: Wiley Blevins
© 2018 Scholastic Inc.

All rights reserved. Published in 2018 by Children's Press, an imprint of Scholastic Inc.
Printed in North Mankato, MN, USA 113
SCHOLASTIC, CHILDREN'S PRESS, and associated logos are trademarks and/or registered trademarks of Scholastic Inc.
Scholastic Inc., 557 Broadway, New York, NY 10012

1 2 3 4 5 6 7 8 9 10 R 27 26 25 24 23 22 21 20 19 18

Photos ©: cover background: narvikk/iStockphoto; cover child: Pando Hall/Getty Images; back cover: Pando Hall/Getty Images; 1: Pando Hall/Getty Images; 3: Elvira Kolomiytseva/Dreamstime; 4 left: Pando Hall/Getty Images; 6: princigalli/iStockphoto; 7 left: Halfdark/Getty Images; 7 right: Prisma Bildagentur/UIG/Getty Images; 8 left: Becker & Bredel/ullstein bild/Getty Images; 8 top center left: Paul Cowan/Dreamstime; 8 top center right: Jack Jelly/Shutterstock; 8 top right: TinasDreamworld/iStockphoto; 9: FoodPhotogr. Eising/age fotostock; 10: Armin Floreth/imageBROKER/age fotostock; 11: Siegfried Kuttig/imageBROKER/age fotostock; 12 bottom: Maciej Es/Shutterstock; 12-13 background: Vadim Yerofeyev/Dreamstime; 13 top: Maciej Es/Shutterstock; 13 bottom: Maciej Es/Shutterstock; 14 top left: minnystock/Dreamstime; 14 top right: Karelian/Shutterstock; 14 bottom: Elvira Kolomiytseva/Dreamstime; 15 top: Andreas_Zerndl/iStockphoto; 15 bottom: koufax73/iStockphoto; 16 top left: Aflo Photo Agency/age fotostock; 16 top right: Christian Horz/Shutterstock; 16 bottom: Riccardo Sala/age fotostock; 17 left: NickolayV/iStockphoto; 17 right: Nikada/iStockphoto; 18 left: Photo 12/Archives Snark/Alamy Images; 18 center: Keystone-France/Gamma-Keystone/Getty Images; 18 right: Pictorial Press Ltd/Alamy Images; 19 left: Sueddeutsche Zeitung Photo/Alamy Images; 19 center: ullstein bild/The Granger Collection; 19 right: miraba/Shutterstock; 20 left: Image Asset Management/age fotostock; 20 right: AP Images; 21 top: BL/Robana/age fotostock; 21 bottom: Rawpixel.com/Shutterstock; 22 left: Florian Bachmeier/imageBROKER/age fotostock; 22 right: Christian Mueringer/Dreamstime; 23 top left: Mangroove/Dreamstime; 23 center left top: Thomas Imo/Photothek/Getty Images; 23 bottom left: Endress, Angela Franc/age fotostock; 23 center left bottom: Lisa und Wilfried Bahnmüller/Media Bakery; 23 right: ArtCookStudio/Shutterstock; 24 right: Holm Roehner/Bongarts/Getty Images; 24 left: Alex Egorov/Shutterstock; 25: Bodo Marks/picture-alliance/dpa/AP Images; 26 bottom left: Ljupco/iStockphoto; 26 top right: Inara Prusakova/Dreamstime; 26 bottom right: ajafoto/iStockphoto; 26 bottom right: Keystone-France/Gamma-Rapho/Getty Images; 27 top left: RossHelen/iStockphoto; 27 center: Kai Horstmann/age fotostock; 27 bottom left: 360b/Shutterstock; 27 top right: Digital-Fotofusion Gallery/Alamy Images; 27 bottom right: Stefan Puchner/picture-alliance/dpa/AP Images; 28 A: Jürgen Wackenhut/imageBROKER/age fotostock; 28 B: Nikolay Prikhodko/Dreamstime; 28 C: MichaelUtech/iStockphoto; 28 D: Noppasin Wongchum/Dreamstime; 28 E: Nico Stengert/age fotostock; 28 G: Christoph Papsch/age fotostock; 28 F: Daniel Karmann/picture-alliance/dpa/AP Images; 30 right: Paul Stringer/Shutterstock; 30 left: Leontura/iStockphoto; 30 bottom: Pando Hall/Getty Images.

Maps by Jim McMahon.

Table of Contents

Where in the World Is Germany?

Hallo (HAH-loh) from Germany! That's how we say "hello." I'm Johann, and I will be your tour guide. My name is German for "John." Germany is located in central Europe, or the "heart of Europe," as I like to say. My country is made up of 16 different and fascinating states. Let me show you around.

Fast Facts:

- Germany is 137,847 square miles (357,022 square kilometers) in area.

- It has the highest population of any country in Europe, at more than 82 million.

- The name Germany comes from the Latin word *Germania*.

- Germany is the seventh-most visited country by tourists in the world.

- The southern part of Germany is covered by a mountain range called the Alps.

- Germany's main rivers are the Rhine, Elbe, Danube, Mosel, Main, Weser, and Oder.

- The climate in Germany is generally **temperate**, with four seasons. It is cold and often overcast in winter and warm in summer.

Some apartments look out on a courtyard that is full of green.

Last Name	Occupation
Müller	miller (grinds wheat into flour)
Schmidt	smith (works with metal, such as a blacksmith)
Schneider	tailor (makes and fixes clothes)
Fischer	fisher
Weber	weaver (makes cloth or fabrics)
Koch	cook
Meyer	farmer

Home Sweet Home

I am from Berlin, Germany. I live with my parents and older brother in an apartment. Our building has a beautiful **courtyard**. One set of my grandparents lives across the street. The other grandparents live 10 minutes away. Many German families live close to relatives, and family members often gather for big meals.

My last name is Becker, which means that my **ancestors** were bakers. You can tell a lot about someone's ancestors based on their last names. Why? A person's last name often told their occupation, or job. The chart above has some common German last names. Is yours on the list?

Many homes are bright, with a lot of windows.

Bakery

If you visit my home, you might be surprised that we open all our windows a lot—even in winter. We like to air out our homes at least twice a week. That lets in fresh air and keeps **mold** from growing. Other things you'll notice are our small kitchens, the lack of closets, and our special room for the toilet. It's separate from where we wash and bathe.

My family does some of its shopping at outdoor markets scattered around the city. I love to visit the local bakery for a freshly baked treat. There are also large stores where you can buy almost everything—groceries, clothes, toys and games, furniture, TVs, and more. It makes life easy!

Life is also pretty fun. Like most Germans, we like to take lots of family vacations. Recently we've gone to other parts of Germany as well as to Spain.

Pumpernickel

Spätzle

Gingerbread

Let's Eat!

In Germany, our meals are all about meat and potatoes. We eat meat pies, meat dumplings, and all sorts of meat by itself. We are famous for our sausages, called *Wurst*, and have more than 1,200 different kinds! Try as many as you can when you visit.

Common potato side dishes range from potato pancakes to potato salad. Cabbage, carrots, and asparagus make good side dishes, too. We also enjoy a slice of dark bread called *Pumpernickel* with our meals. It's delicious and nutritious!

Various regions across Germany have their own specialties. Bavaria, for example, cooks *Spätzle*, or spaetzle. This is a small dumpling served with meat and covered in gravy, or served with cinnamon and butter as a dessert. If you visit one of our port cities, you can order eel soup. *Doner kebab* is a dish that came to Germany from Turkey. It is lamb or chicken stuffed into pita bread. It is very popular, too!

We love desserts. One of my favorites are gingerbread and *Springerle*, a hard cookie that tastes like licorice. We eat a lot of tarts, too— apple, cherry, and strawberry.

Some foods are named after places in my country. Hamburgers are named after Hamburg!

Many people in Germany eat five small meals a day: early breakfast, late breakfast, lunch, midafternoon snack, and dinner. You won't go hungry here! Lunch is traditionally our largest meal. Then for the evening meal, everyone in my family gathers for cheese, bread, and cold sliced meat. I especially love my mom's *Brezel*, which is a yummy pretzel bread.

German Manners

Here are some things to remember when eating in Germany.

1 If you're meeting someone at home or at a restaurant, be on time. Try not to be more than a few minutes early, and you should never be late.

2 We don't really like to eat with our fingers, so use a fork and knife. That includes when you eat fries and even pizza!

3 Never put your elbows on the table while eating. How rude!

4 Always thank the cook with a simple *"Das schmeckt wunderbar."* This means, "The food tastes wonderful."

5 When you lay your knife and fork beside your plate, it means "I'm done." Someone will see it and take your plate away!

9

A Schultüte

Off to School

In Germany, we start school at age 6. Our elementary school is called *Grundschule*. My school is so close to my home that I ride my bike there. I'm lucky to go to school with my best friend, Oskar.

On the first day of school, each student gets a large cardboard cone called a *Schultüte*. Families decorate it and fill it with candy, toys, and school supplies, which we take with us to class.

At about age 12, our grades from Grundschule or our parents determine which school we'll attend next. We'll stay at that school until we're 18. Our top students go to a *Gymnasium*. Before they graduate, they take an important test to be accepted into colleges. *Realschule* and *Hauptschule* students study subjects that prepare them to go to either a college or a vocational (trade) school.

Freund
(froind)

friend

Most of our lessons are taught in German, our official language. German is also spoken in many countries around Germany, such as Austria, Belgium, northern Italy, Luxembourg, and Switzerland. We study English as a second language in my school. Most people in Germany speak more than one language.

Learn Some German Slang!

Alles Banana = "Everything is banana," which means "Everything is fine."

Mir schwillt der Kamm = "My comb is swelling," which means "I'm getting angry!"

Hier ist tote Hose = "Here it's dead pants," which means "Here it's boring."

Knowing how to count to 10 is important when you visit Germany. Study hard and *viel Glück* (good luck)!

1	**eins**	*(EYENTS)*
2	**zwei**	*(TSVY)*
3	**drei**	*(DRY)*
4	**vier**	*(FEER)*
5	**fünf**	*(FOONF)*
6	**sechs**	*(ZECKS)*
7	**sieben**	*(ZEE-ben)*
8	**acht**	*(AHKT)*
9	**neun**	*(NOYN)*
10	**zehn**	*(TSAYN)*

The Pied Piper of Hamelin

In school, we read a lot of folktales, fairy tales, and **legends** from long ago. The Grimm Brothers (Jacob and Wilhelm) lived in Germany in the early 1800s. They collected and wrote many of these well-known tales, such as Snow White, Rapunzel, and Puss in Boots. One of my favorites is the legend of the Pied Piper of Hamelin.

Long ago, the town of Hamelin had a big problem: Rats, rats, and more rats! The town was overrun with them. One day, a man dressed in multicolored (or *pied*) clothes and playing a pipe strolled into town. "I can get rid of these rats," he said. "But only if you pay me 1,000 gold coins." It was a large sum.

But the mayor was desperate for a solution, so he agreed to pay it. The Pied Piper played a beautiful tune on his pipe. All the town's rats were captivated. They followed the man out of town like they were under a spell. He tricked the rats into going into the rushing waters of the river. And there they all drowned.

When the Pied Piper went to the mayor to collect his money, the mayor refused. "It's too much," he said. Angry, the piper vowed to get even. One day, he snuck into town when the adults were at a meeting. The piper played a special song on his pipe. All the town's children were attracted to its sweet tune. They followed the man out of town until they came to a big rock in the mountains. The Pied Piper led them into a deep cave inside the rock. The children were never seen again. To this day, people wonder about the strange magic in that Pied Piper's pipe.

Brandenburg Gate

Tiergarten Park

Touring Germany

Berlin: Capital City

Welcome to my city, Berlin. It's the capital of Germany and our biggest city. When you visit, first check out the Brandenburg Gate. This was once the city's official entrance. After that, head over to the Berlin Wall. This wall once split the city in two. Only a small section remains.

We use bikes, trains, and cars to travel around my city. The **subway** is the *Untergrundbahn*, or "underground train." We call it the *U-Bahn*. The aboveground train is the *S-Bahn*, which is short for *Schnellbahn*, or "fast train."

Once you know how you'll travel, grab a map and visit two of my favorite sites. One is the large and beautiful Charlottenburg Palace. The other is Tiergarten Park. Rent a bike and visit the zoo or one of the many small lakes there. While in Berlin, look for statues of colorful bears. The bear is the symbol of Berlin.

Bear statue in Berlin

Black Forest

The Black Forest

If you're ready for a change of scenery, hop on the train and explore one of our famous forests. Germany has more forests than any other country in Europe. Many Germans, including me, like walking through the woods, and many of our folktales take place in them. Just think of Red Riding Hood!

My favorite forest is the Black Forest. Its name comes from the dark evergreen fir trees that fill it. It also has other trees, including walnut trees. Our famous German cuckoo clocks are made from the wood of walnut trees. Buy one and every hour a bird will pop out, making a loud noise. Of course, this could drive your parents cuckoo, too!

Cuckoo clock

Autobahn

A boat travels along a channel between warehouses in Hamburg.

Other Fun Places to Visit

You can travel around Germany on the *Autobahn*, our highway system. Most of it has no speed limits for cars and motorcycles. That's right—you can go as fast as you want. Zoom!

Three-fourths of all Germans live in cities. Hamburg is our second-largest city. It is located in northern Germany. It's an important port, so be ready to see lots of boats and eat yummy seafood. The model railway museum there is the biggest in the world.

Munich is our third-largest city. It's located in Bavaria in southern Germany. Munich holds a big **festival** each year called Oktoberfest. Visitors come from all over the world to enjoy it. The one thing you'll notice about this city is the decorated clocks. They are everywhere—on gates, church steeples, old towers, and more. Play a game with your family to see who can spot the most!

Clock in Munich

Roman ruins in Cologne

Medieval buildings in Frankfurt

Cologne sits on the Rhine River and is our fourth-largest city. The ancient Romans settled this city more than 2,000 years ago. Travel around and you can still see ancient Roman ruins. You've probably heard this city's name before. It's another name for perfume.

One additional city you shouldn't miss is Frankfurt. Any city that has a food named after it must be fun! This city has a mix of very tall, modern buildings and **medieval** streets. Even if you don't visit the city, you'll probably fly through it. It has one of the busiest airports in the world. But be warned—if you are transferring from one plane to another, leave plenty of time. The airport is huge. It takes a long time to get from one place to another. If you miss your plane, don't worry too much. You can take a "behind the scenes" airport tour to see how the airport works while waiting for your next flight.

Our Country's History

People have lived on this land for about 10,000 years. We have had a very rich history. However, in the early 20th century, one of the darkest ages of our country started. At the time, many people could not find jobs. They had trouble affording food and clothing. Adolf Hitler and other Germans believed the hateful and false idea that Jewish people were to blame. In 1933, Hitler became the leader of Germany. His army was

Timeline: Key Moments in German History

Roman coin

Charlemagne

57 BCE

Roman Empire
Some of Germany becomes part of the Roman Empire, an ancient empire that, at its largest, spanned from Britain to western Asia.

768–814 CE

Charlemagne (Franks)
Charlemagne, King of the Franks (a group of people originally from our territory), rules much of Europe.

Early 1800s

German Confederation
Thirty-nine independent German-speaking states come together to create a single economy.

1871

Wilhelm I
The first kaiser (ruler) unites Germany into a single country.

1914–1918

World War I
Germany fights in this worldwide conflict that involves more than 30 nations.

brutal and invaded many neighboring countries, leading to a conflict known as World War II (1939–1945). He killed millions of innocent people in harsh prison camps called concentration camps. The victims included Jewish people, the disabled, Roma (Gypsies), and anyone else Hitler's followers considered "lesser." We do not want something that terrible to happen again. At the end of the war, Germany and Hitler were defeated.

German Soldiers in World War II

The Berlin Wall

The German Flag

1939–1945

World War II
The Axis Powers (Germany, Italy, and Japan) are defeated by the Allies (the United States, Great Britain, France, and other countries). Germany splits into two countries: West Germany and East Germany.

1950s

European Integration
West German leaders resume a friendly relationship with the U.S. The countries become strong allies.

1961–1989

Berlin Wall
A huge wall is built to separate East Berlin from West Berlin. It is torn down in 1989 and East and West Germany reunite a year later.

1990 onwards

Modern Germany
Germany is a strong country and a very important member of the European Union, an organization of 28 European nations.

It Came From Germany

My country is known as the birthplace of many famous classical music **composers**. These include Ludwig van Beethoven, Wolfgang Amadeus Mozart, Johann Sebastian Bach, Johannes Brahms, George Frideric Handel, and Richard Wagner. You should find and listen to their amazing music.

My favorite composer is Beethoven. He wrote his first important piece of music at age 12, but sadly went deaf when he was 26 years old. Yet he still wrote music by "hearing" it in his head. Wow!

We have also produced many famous scientists. You've probably heard of the genius Albert Einstein. He was born here and is known as the father of modern physics. That's the study of matter and energy. He is most famous for his equation $E = mc^2$. Maybe you'll study that someday! In 1932, he left Germany for the United States, where he continued his research.

Some of the first and most important books were printed in Germany. In the 1400s, Johannes Gutenberg invented a new way of making books using movable type on a printing press. Instead of carving out huge blocks of type for each page, he made small blocks—one for each letter. The letters could be rearranged to make words. This invention changed the world by making books faster, easier, and cheaper to print. As a result, books became more available for people who weren't rich enough to afford books before. Gutenberg is famous for printing beautiful editions of the Bible.

Did you go to kindergarten? Guess what? It was invented in Germany! The word *kindergarten* means "children's garden." When kindergarten started, the children were thought of as plants. The teacher was the "gardener" who "watered" them with the knowledge needed to help them grow.

Children perform a traditional dance in lederhosen and dirndls at a festival in Kreuth.

Christmas tree

Celebrate!

Everyone loves a holiday, and we have some fun ones in Germany. During some holidays, we dress up in traditional costumes. For example, you might spot boys wearing leather pants called *Lederhosen* and girls in colorful skirts called *Dirndls* in southern parts of the country.

Christmas is my favorite holiday. You'll spot tons of Christmas markets across Germany. You can buy wooden toys, hand-carved music boxes, and glass tree ornaments. We usually decorate our Christmas trees with these ornaments, silvery strands of "angel hair," and white candles. But we have one warning: It is bad luck for kids to see the tree before Christmas Eve. When my parents have decorated our tree, they ring a special bell. Then my brother and I rush in to see it!

It takes days for my parents to prepare the traditional Christmas meal. The feast includes roasted goose, a sweet fruit bread called stollen, and lots of yummy cookies.

September–October

Other Fun Celebrations

Oktoberfest: This is one of the world's biggest outdoor festivals. Pretzels and wursts galore! Despite its name, this holiday starts in September.

October

German Unity Day: This celebrates the day in 1990 when West and East Germany reunited.

November

Saint Martin's Day: This day celebrates the saint of children and the poor. Kids go door-to-door singing and carrying lanterns. At each home they receive candy or small toys.

December

Saint Nicholas Day: On this day, kids get big bags of candy in honor of this gift-giving saint.

Make a Potato Pancake

Ask an adult to help!

Ingredients:
4 potatoes; 1 onion; 1 egg; 2 tablespoons flour; 1/4 teaspoon salt; 1/4 teaspoon black pepper; 1 tablespoon olive oil; sour cream and/or applesauce

1. **Preheat** the oven to 400°F.

2. **Shred** the potatoes and onion with a box grater. **Place** the shredded food in a colander and **push** down on it, squeezing out moisture.

3. **Beat** the egg. Combine the egg, potatoes, and onion in a large bowl.

4. **Mix** in flour, salt, and pepper.

5. **Put** parchment paper on a baking sheet. **Spread** the oil on the parchment paper.

6. **Form** the potato mix into 8 flat pancakes. **Place** them on the parchment paper.

7. **Bake** for 20 to 25 minutes, or until golden brown.

   Serve with sour cream or applesauce, and enjoy!

23

Skiing

Soccer

Time to Play

Kids in Germany love sports. Germans tend to be very **athletic** people. About one-third of us belong to sports clubs. And what do we love to play most? Soccer, of course! It's our national sport. We play soccer wherever and whenever we can. Both our men's and women's national teams have won the World Cup soccer tournament several times.

Other sports we enjoy are Formula One motor racing, tennis, basketball, cycling, gymnastics, and volleyball. We also love anything outdoors, such as hiking and camping in our many forests. If you're feeling even more adventurous, head up into our beautiful mountains called the Alps. While there, you can put on some skis or hop on a snowboard and enjoy the snow!

The first player to get all of their pieces to the end row wins *Mensch ärgere Dich nicht.*

A popular kids' game in Germany is a board game called *Mensch ärgere Dich nicht*, or Don't Get Annoyed. Why? If a player's game piece lands on your piece, you have to go back to START. Ugh! The game is almost 100 years old. Each player tosses a die and moves his or her game piece around the cross-shaped pattern on the game board. This game is similar to the American game Sorry! It is a ton of fun!

25

You Won't Believe This!

Germans have invented a lot of things: automobile, clarinet, jet engine, motorcycle, Christmas tree, teddy bear, garden gnome, aspirin, and Chinese checkers, to name a few. But my favorite is the gummy bear.

Whether a child is a boy or girl will be clear by the name. Why? The government has to approve all baby names. Odd or unclear names, such as Apple or Bubbles, are not allowed.

The German word for pretzel is *Brezel*. This comes from the Latin word for "bracelet" or "little arm." The shape of a pretzel is meant to look like the crossed arms of someone praying. In the 1600s, children wore pretzel necklaces for good luck.

It is considered bad luck in Germany to wish someone happy birthday before the night of his or her birthday. The person could have a bad day, or worse!

College education in Germany is free, even for people from other countries. So brush up on your German and get a free education here!

The chancellor's office in Berlin is known as the Washing Machine because of the way it looks. It's a huge, square, concrete building with a large glass circle at the front.

The Berlin Zoo has more species than any other zoo in the world. Germany also has more than 400 other zoos. They include wildlife parks, aquariums, bird parks, animal reserves, and safari parks.

We have more than 300 different kinds of bread in Germany. We love it so much we even have a bread museum in Ulm. The museum is dedicated to the 6,000-year history of this favorite food.

Our first female chancellor (political leader of Germany), Angela Merkel, was first elected in 2005. She is so popular that a Barbie doll was made to look like her!

Guessing Game!

Here are some other great sites around Germany. If you have time, try to see them all!

Use the elevated walkway to get the best view of this forest located in Hainich National Park.

E

A

This area is the world's first nature reserve and was formed by volcanic activity.

1. Lake Constance
2. Wildcat Children's Forest
3. Spielzeugmuseum
4. Neuschwanstein Castle
5. Drachenfels
6. Cologne Cathedral
7. Schokoladen Museum

F

Nuremberg is home to this toy museum, which will bring out the kid in everyone.

B

A favorite spot for families to visit, you can also walk, bike, kayak, or boat to Switzerland and Austria from here.

D

King Ludwig II built this magical-looking castle, which inspired Sleeping Beauty's castle at Disneyland. Can you see the resemblance?

This chocolate museum in Cologne will make any visitor hungry.

G

This cathedral, with super high ceilings and pointy arches, is one of the world's most famous churches.

C

28

Preparing for Your Visit

By now, you should be ready to hop on a plane to Germany. Here are some tips to prepare for your trip.

1 Before you come to Germany, exchange your money. Our money is called the euro. Many members of the European Union, like us, use this money. You'll need some euros to buy fun souvenirs.

2 If you want a nice drive, take a long trip down the 200-mile (322 km) Romantic Road. It runs all the way from Würzburg to Füssen. You will see the most beautiful scenery in my country along the way.

3 If you want to travel by train, hop on the Deutsche Bahn. Kids under 15 travel for free if they're with a parent or grandparent. We even have high-speed bullet trains that can go as fast as 186 miles (300 km) per hour. Whoosh!

4 Bring a pair of binoculars. These will allow you to zoom in on a faraway castle in the mountains or animals moving through a forest as you travel.

5 When you're traveling outside the large cities, I recommend staying at a farm or at one of our hay hotels. A hay hotel is a special barn for travelers where you actually sleep on a bed of hay!

6 Bring a converter for your electronics. Outlets have a different shape in Europe than in the United States. A converter is a special plug designed to connect your electronics into any outlet!

The United States Compared to Germany

Official Name	United States of America (USA)	Federal Republic of Germany (Deutschland)
Official Language	No official language, though English is most commonly used	German
Population	325 million	82 million
Common Words	yes; no; thank you	ja (ya); nein (nine); danke (DAHN-kah)
Flag		
Money	Dollar	Euro
Location	North America	Central Europe
Highest Point	Denali (Mount McKinley)	Zugspitze on the Austrian border
Lowest Point	Death Valley	In Neuendorf bei Wilster in northern Germany
National Anthem	"The Star-Spangled Banner"	"Deutschlandlied"

So now you know some important and fascinating things about my country, Germany. I hope to see you someday hiking in one of our beautiful forests, exploring one of our historic cities, or feasting on some of our tasty foods. Until then . . . *auf Wiedersehen* (owf VEE-der-zay-en). Good-bye!

Glossary

ancestors
(AN-ses-turz)
members of a family who lived long ago

athletic
(ath-LET-ik)
trained in or good at sports and exercise

centuries
(SEN-chur-eez)
periods of 100 years

composers
(kuhm-POH-zurz)
people who write something, especially music

courtyard
(KORT-yahrd)
an open area surrounded by walls or buildings

festival
(FES-tuh-vuhl)
a celebration or holiday

legends
(LEJ-uhndz)
stories handed down from earlier times

medieval
(mee-DEE-vuhl)
of or having to do with the Middle Ages (about 1000 to 1450 CE)

mold
(MOHLD)
a kind of organism that grows on things that are warm and moist

subway
(SUHB-way)
an electric train or a system of trains that runs underground in a city

temperate
(TEM-pur-it)
describing a climate in which the temperature is rarely very high or very low

Index

Facts for Now

Visit this Scholastic website for more information on Germany and to download the Teaching Guide for this series:

www.factsfornow.scholastic.com Enter the keyword **Germany**

About the Author

Wiley Blevins is an author living and working in New York City. His greatest love is traveling. He has been to Germany many times and learned to speak some German in high school. He has written several books for children, including the Ick and Crud series and the Scary Tales Retold series.